Introduction to Written Japanese

Hiragana

Jim Gleeson

ひらがな

CHARLES E. TUTTLE COMPANY
Rutland, Vermont & Tokyo, Japan

Visit Tuttle Web on the Internet at:
http://www.tuttle.co.jp/~tuttle/

Published by the Charles E. Tuttle Company, Inc.
of Rutland, Vermont & Tokyo, Japan
with editorial offices at
Suido 1-chome, 2-6, Bunkyo-ku, Tokyo 112

LCC 96-60248
ISBN 0-8048-2075-9

First Edition, 1996

Illustrations by Michelle Ker
Printed in Singapore

It is widely accepted that students of Japanese progress more quickly if they learn the written component of the language at an early stage of their studies. Unfortunately, many students are daunted by the task of learning a large number of seemingly complex characters.

The complexity of Japanese characters, however is something of an illusion, for many of the characters are merely combinations of comparatively few elements. This fact becomes apparent as one progresses through the two forty-six character syllabaries, known collectively as kana, and the two thousand or so kanji characters that are used in written Japanese today.

Anybody who is able to master English, with its irregular spellings and idiosyncratic pronunciations, is more than equipped to master written Japanese.

The hiragana and katakana syllabaries are purely phonetic characters, which function much like the letters of the English alphabet. In this respect, kana are quite different from kanji characters, which are based on Chinese ideographs. The basic function of hiragana is to supplement the kanji.

Generally, kanji are used to represent the ideas in a sentence while hiragana are used to represent the relationships between the ideas. For example, whereas the concept of 'go' would be written in kanji, hiragana would be suffixed to the kanji to indicate 'want to go', 'went', 'will not go', and so forth. Hiragana is also used for particles such as 'to', 'in', 'by', and 'at'. Katakana are most often used for words of foreign origin.

Each of the hiragana and katakana syllabaries represent all of the sounds in spoken Japanese. Unlike kanji, which can take on a variety of pronunciations according to their context, the pronunciation of the kana characters is quite regular. Although it is possible to write Japanese using only hiragana, a native Japanese speaker would find it somewhat difficult to understand. Kanji are used for clarity, eloquence, and immediacy of meaning. It is customary for the student to write using only hiragana at first, then to substitute kanji into their writing as they are learned.

Japanese schoolchildren learn their characters by writing them out, and this is generally acknowledged as the fastest way to master them.

This book has been prepared so that students at the introductory level of Japanese can become acquainted

は
じ
め
に

with the written component of the language in the quickest possible way. The overriding priority has been given to active student involvement, with a variety of practice sentences and expressions provided to reinforce the characters learned at each stage of progress. The book also features grayed-out, trace-over characters to enable the student to gain the correct feel and balance of each character.

To avoid repetition, this book uses the dictionary form of verbs rather than the ~*masu* form. In the majority of situations, however, it is customary to write using the ~*masu* form.

This book uses the Hepburn system of Romanization. It is important to remember, however, that Japanese is a separate language with an independent set of sounds to English, and hence, any attempt to Romanize it can only be an approximation.

The author would like to thank the following people for their invaluable assistance: Miyuki Habara, practice examples, general advice, Shigeo Tokikuni, proofreading, historical research; Makoto Habara, typographic research; Taiji Habara, Japanese font uploading software; Yoshie Sasaki, practice examples; Michael Priest, scanning, 3D mapping, technical support; Kiyo Nakazawa, historical research; Tom Kent, general support and assistance; Carmel de Jager, additional research.

Contents ■■

もくじ

In both printed and handwritten Japanese, the characters occupy imaginary squares of equal size, with each character centered within its square.

All of the writing practice in this book involves writing characters within squares, and the squares have centerlines to provide the correct balance and feel for writing Japanese.

Traditionally, Japanese is written with a brush or *fude*, and this fact is reflected in many typographic styles today. Although the *fude* is no longer widely used, some principles of using a *fude* still apply to writing Japanese with a pencil or ballpoint pen – in particular, the stroke endings.

The strokes of Japanese characters terminate in one of three ways, as illustrated below.

i) Jumping, to produce a hook at the end of the stroke. This ending is called *hane*, from the verb *haneru*, to jump.
ii) Bringing the pen or pencil to a stop while it is on the page. This ending is called *tome*, from the verb *tomeru*, to stop.
iii) Lifting the pen or pencil off the page while it is moving. This ending is called *harai*, meaning "sweep."

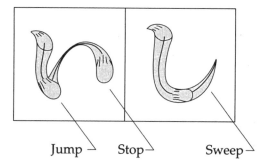

When tracing over the characters, be sure to keep these three types of stroke endings in mind, observing how the strokes of the gray-tinted characters terminate.

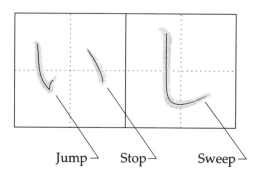

In Japanese as in English, there are many differences between handwritten and typeset characters. To enable students to gain the correct feel for written Japanese, educators in Japan have developed a neutral typeface which incorporates the features of handwritten Japanese without the stylistic idiosyncracies of any individual.

This typeface is known simply as Schoolbook or *Kyō-kasho*, and is the standard typeface used to teach Japanese schoolchildren their written language. All of the practice characters in this book are set in *Kyōkasho*.

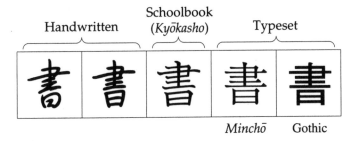

To provide familiarity with a range of type variations, each character entry in this book is accompanied by four different character styles, as shown below. These variations are included for recognition only.

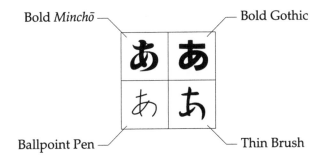

The upper left variation is a bold *Minchō* typeface while the upper right variation is a bold Gothic typeface. Typefaces of this kind are frequently used in advertisements and newspaper headlines.

The lower left typeface simulates the characters written with a ballpoint pen, while the lower right typeface is a thin brush script indicative of that used on traditional occasions.

In around 100 A.D., Chinese characters, known as kanji, entered Japan via the Korean peninsula. Since that time, many thousands of kanji have come to Japan, many of them falling into disuse or becoming obsolete. Today, there are about two thousand kanji in general use, with several thousand more being used on special or formal occasions.

Although kanji refer to ideas or objects, by around 800 A.D., a special set of kanji had evolved which were used for their pronunciation, with the innate meaning of the characters being discarded.

In the Heian period (794–1185), these characters underwent a series of simplifications and reductions via calligraphy, which was widely practiced by the aristocracy.

The result was a simple, cursive set of characters known as hiragana. Unlike kanji, which refer to ideas or objects and which can take on a variety of pronunciations according to their context, each hiragana character is pronounced in only one way, and there is no conceptual meaning.

A chart showing the evolution of all the hiragana characters is given inside the back cover.

1500 B.C.	Chinese tortoise shell inscription
202 B.C.	Chinese Han period
C100 A.D.	Kanji enter Japan.
350 A.D.	Kanji in wide-spread use
540 A.D.	Buddhism comes to Japan.
794 A.D.	Heike clan comes to power. Kyoto established as imperial capital.
Heian period	Various art forms flourish.
1185 A.D.	Heike clan defeated in battle.

Hiragana evolves through cursive brush script.

Kanji

Hiragana

| Present | Character forms remain virtually unchanged after Heian period. |

ひらがな

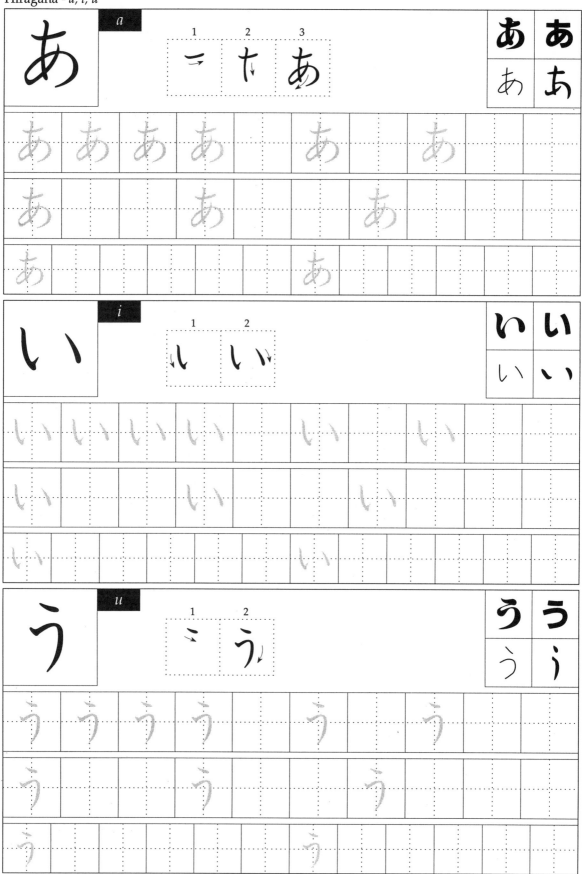

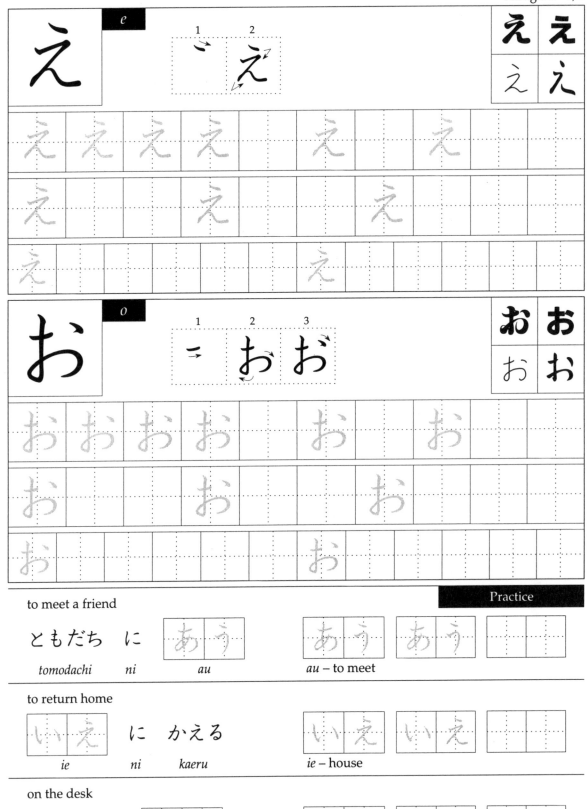

e

1 2

o

1 2 3

to meet a friend

ともだち に

tomodachi   *ni*   *au*

au – to meet

to return home

に かえる

ie   *ni*   *kaeru*

ie – house

on the desk

つくえ の

tsukue   *no*   *ue*

ue – above, up, on

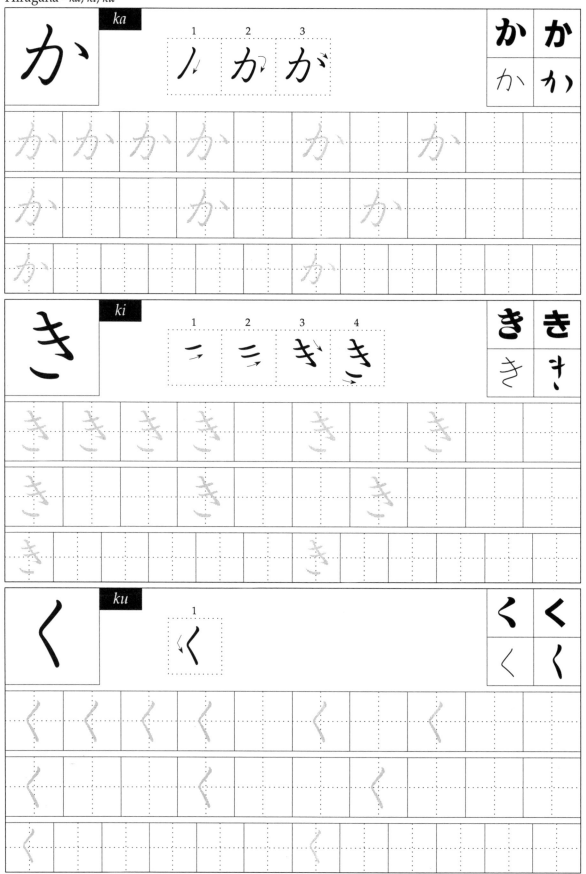

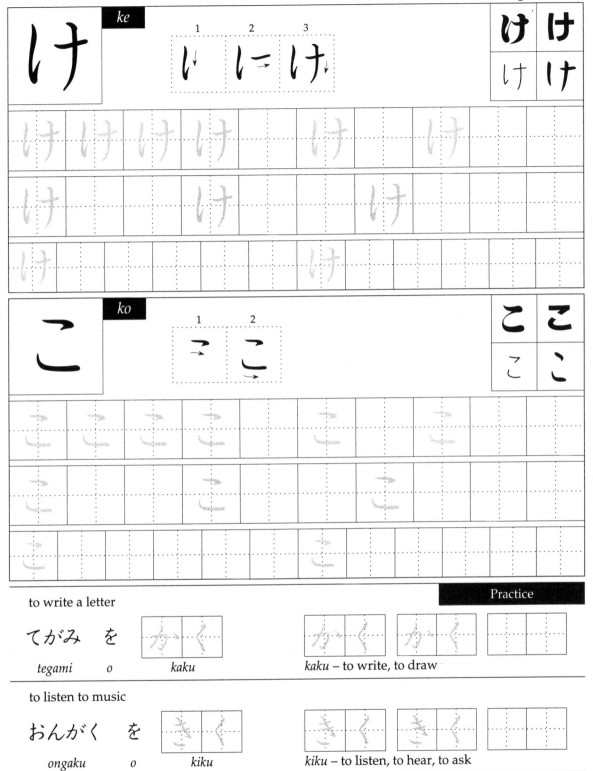

け *ke*

| 1 | 2 | 3 |

こ *ko*

| 1 | 2 |

Practice

to write a letter

てがみ を　かく

tegami　o　kaku

kaku – to write, to draw

to listen to music

おんがく を　きく

ongaku　o　kiku

kiku – to listen, to hear, to ask

It is here.

ここ　です。

Koko　desu.

koko – here

13

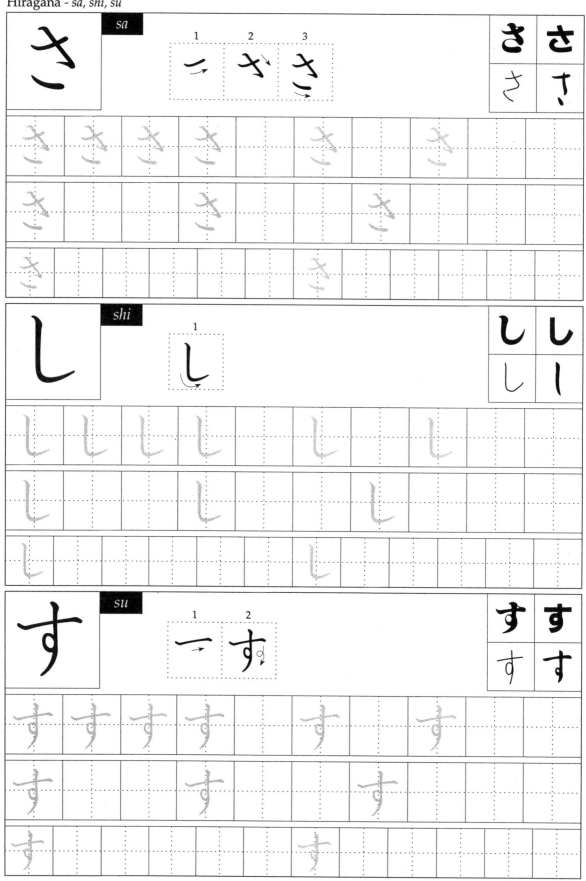

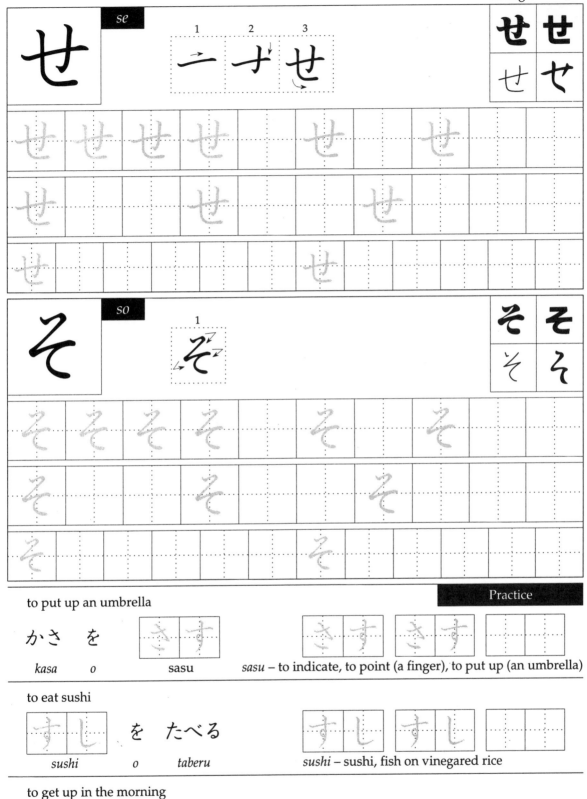

se

1 2 3

so

1

Practice

to put up an umbrella

かさ を さす

kasa *o* *sasu*

sasu – to indicate, to point (a finger), to put up (an umbrella)

to eat sushi

すし を たべる

sushi *o* *taberu*

sushi – sushi, fish on vinegared rice

to get up in the morning

あさ おきる

asa *okiru*

asa – morning

I speak loudly.

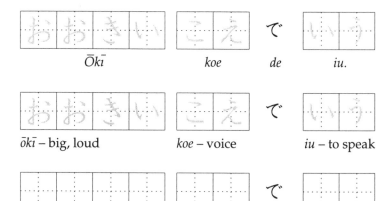

Ōkī   koe   de   iu.

ōkī – big, loud   *koe* – voice   *iu* – to speak

The cow eats the grass.

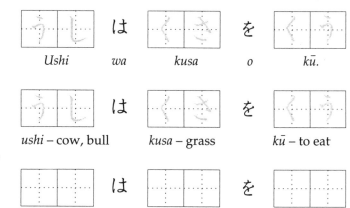

Ushi   wa   kusa   o   kū.

ushi – cow, bull   *kusa* – grass   *kū* – to eat

The squid has lots of legs.

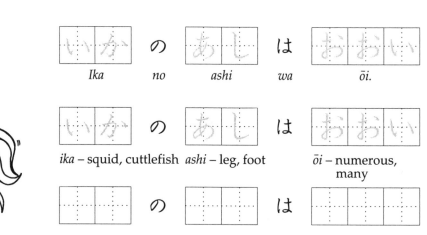

Ika   no   ashi   wa   ōi.

ika – squid, cuttlefish   *ashi* – leg, foot   *ōi* – numerous, many

I'll put the chair over there.

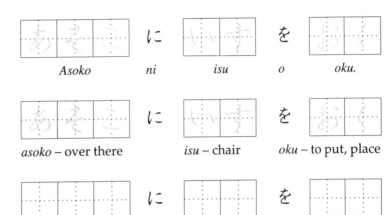

Asoko ni isu o oku.

asoko – over there   *isu* – chair   *oku* – to put, place

I'll go swimming tomorrow.

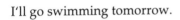

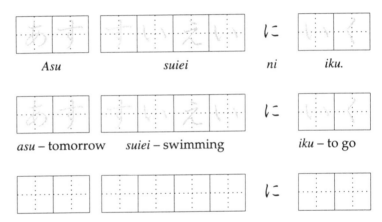

Asu suiei ni iku.

asu – tomorrow   *suiei* – swimming   *iku* – to go

I'll buy some candy at the station.

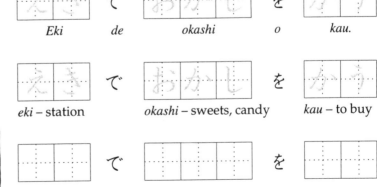

Eki de okashi o kau.

eki – station   *okashi* – sweets, candy   *kau* – to buy

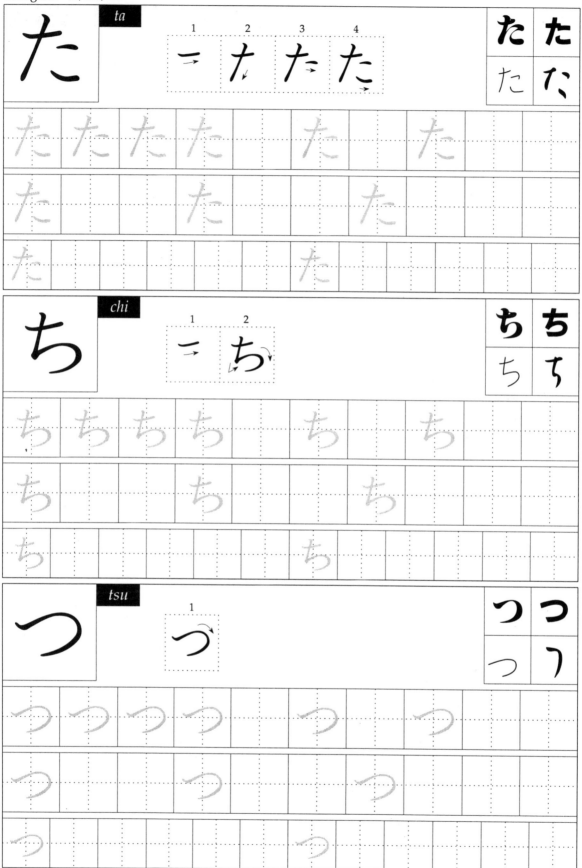

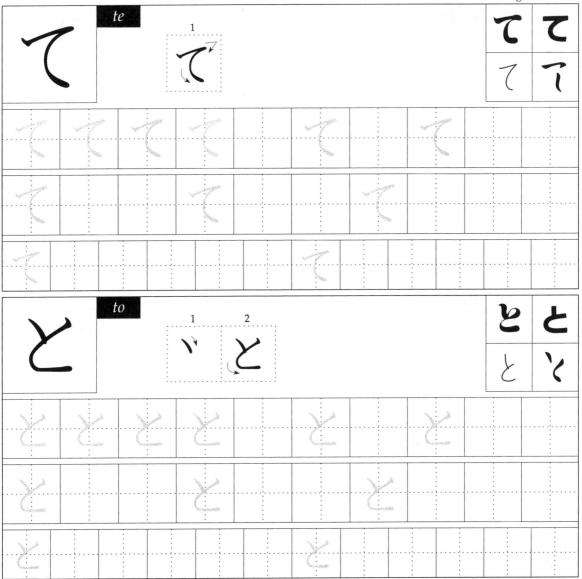

The character *tsu* つ is sometimes written smaller than the surrounding text. In such cases, *tsu* indicates a glottal stop, which is a brief pause in the middle of a word and which has the effect of emphasizing the subsequent consonant. A glottal stop is romanized by the doubling of the subsequent character.

The Glottal Stop – っ

gakkō – school

がっこう

Practice

to stand next to the chair

いす　の　よこ　に　

isu　　*no*　　*yoko*　　*ni*　　　*tatsu*

tatsu – to stand, to rise

It is dirty.

　が　ついている。

Tsuchi　　　*ga*　　　*tsuite iru.*

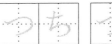

tsuchi – earth, soil, the ground

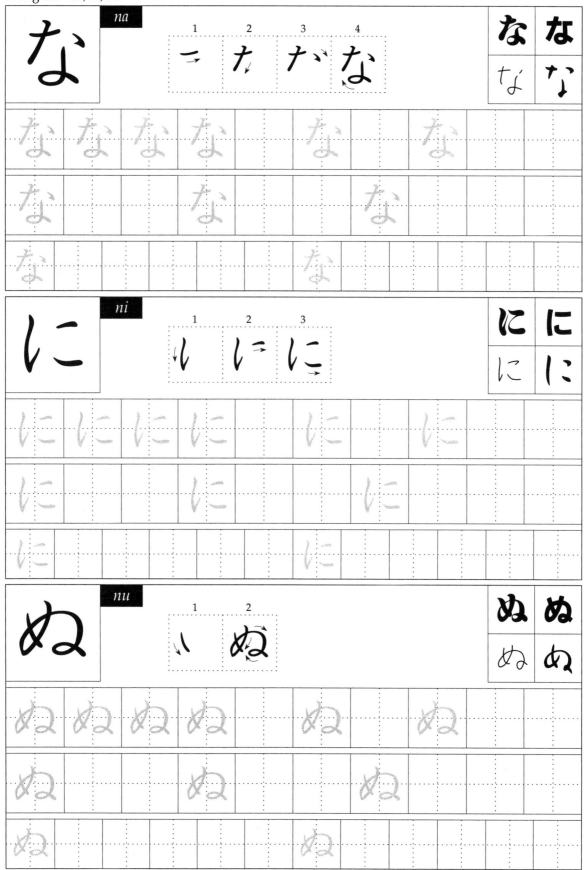

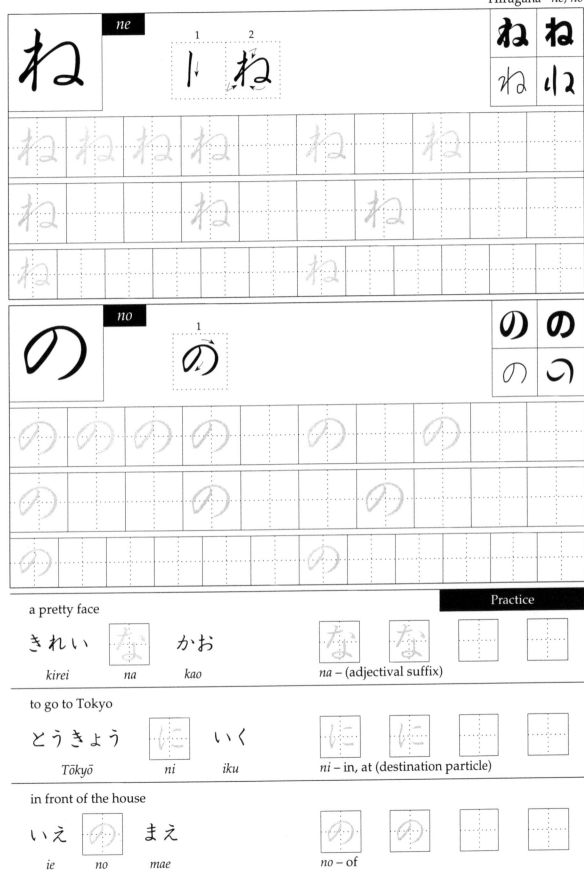

ne

1 2
ト ね

ね ね
ね に

no

1
の

の の
の つ

Practice

a pretty face

きれい　な　かお

kirei　*na*　*kao*

な　な

na – (adjectival suffix)

to go to Tokyo

とうきょう　に　いく

Tōkyō　*ni*　*iku*

に　に

ni – in, at (destination particle)

in front of the house

いえ　の　まえ

ie　*no*　*mae*

の　の

no – of

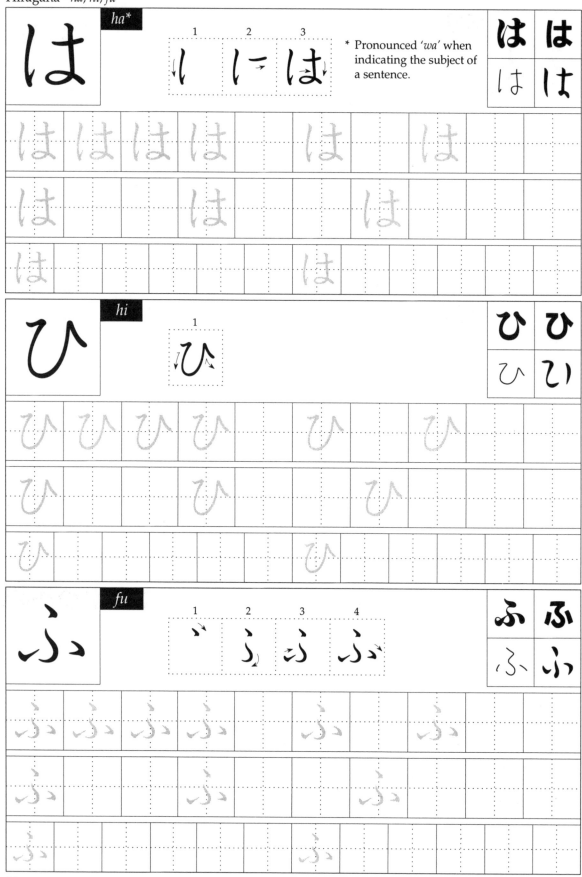

は **ha***

* Pronounced '*wa*' when indicating the subject of a sentence.

ひ *hi*

ふ *fu*

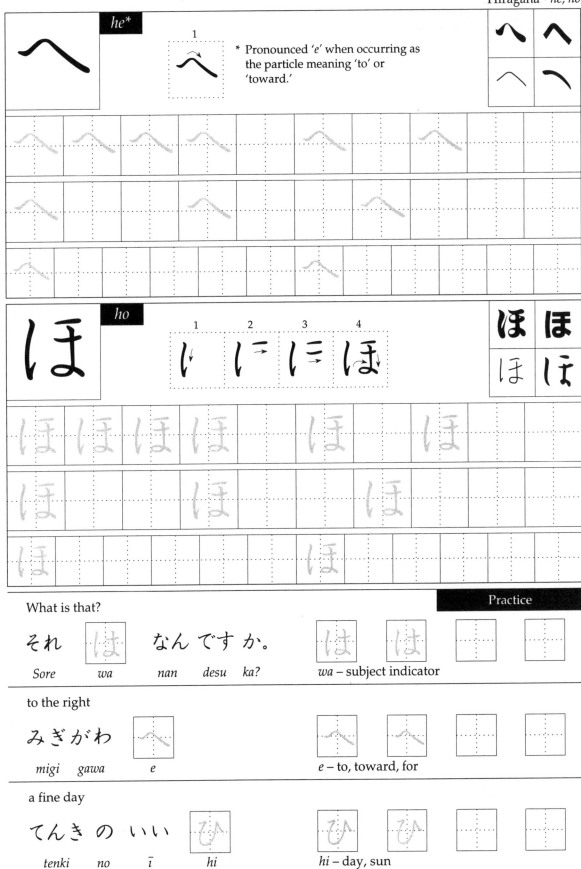

he*

* Pronounced '*e*' when occurring as the particle meaning 'to' or 'toward.'

ho

Practice

What is that?

それ　は　なん　です　か。

Sore　*wa*　*nan*　*desu*　*ka?*

wa – subject indicator

to the right

みぎがわ

migi　*gawa*　*e*

e – to, toward, for

a fine day

てんき　の　いい

tenki　*no*　*ī*　*hi*

hi – day, sun

A tall person

せ	い		が	た	か	い		ひ	と	

sei   *ga*   *takai*   *hito*

せ	い		が	た	か	い		ひ	と	

sei – height, stature   *takai* – tall, high, expensive   *hito* – person

			が							

A short person

せ	い		が	ひ	く	い		ひ	と	

sei   *ga*   *hikui*   *hito*

せ	い		が	ひ	く	い		ひ	と	

sei – height, stature   *hikui* – short, low   *hito* – person

			が							

Fat legs, skinny legs

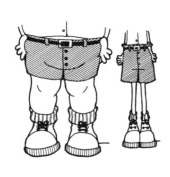

ふ	と	い		あ	し		ほ	そ	い		あ	し	

futoi   *ashi*   *hosoi*   *ashi*

ふ	と	い		あ	し		ほ	そ	い		あ	し	

futoi – large in diameter   *ashi* – leg, foot   *hosoi* – small in diameter

A small airplane

chīsa-na

hikōki

chīsa-na – small

hikōki – airplane

I beat a red drum.

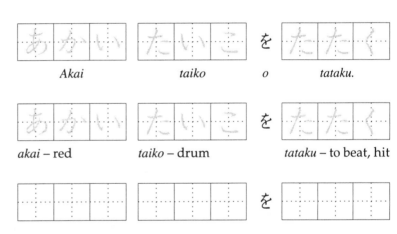

Akai　*taiko*　*o*　*tataku.*

akai – red　*taiko* – drum　*tataku* – to beat, hit

を

A cat in a box

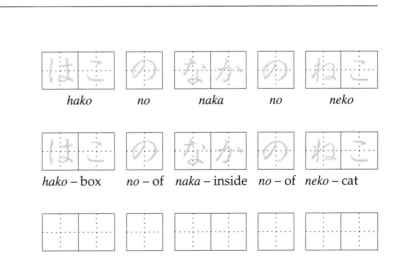

hako　*no*　*naka*　*no*　*neko*

hako – box　*no* – of　*naka* – inside　*no* – of　*neko* – cat

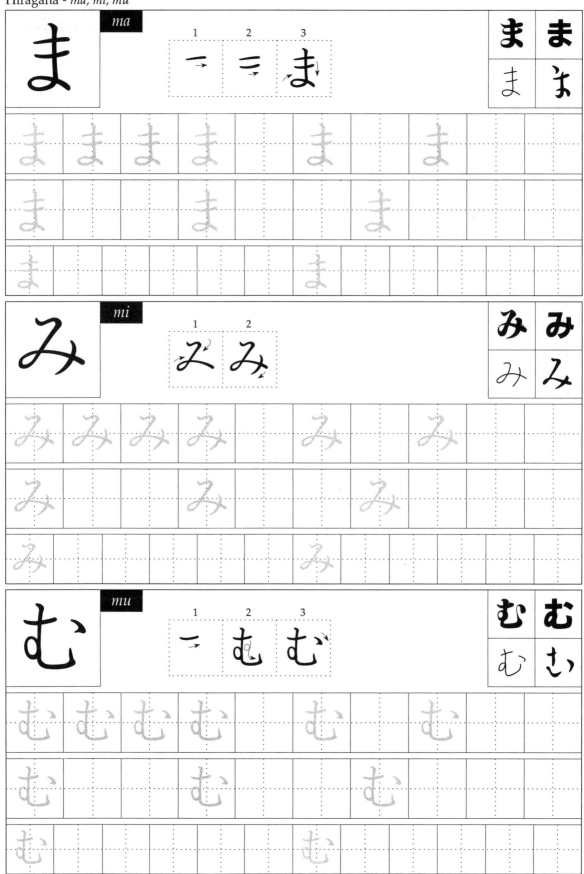

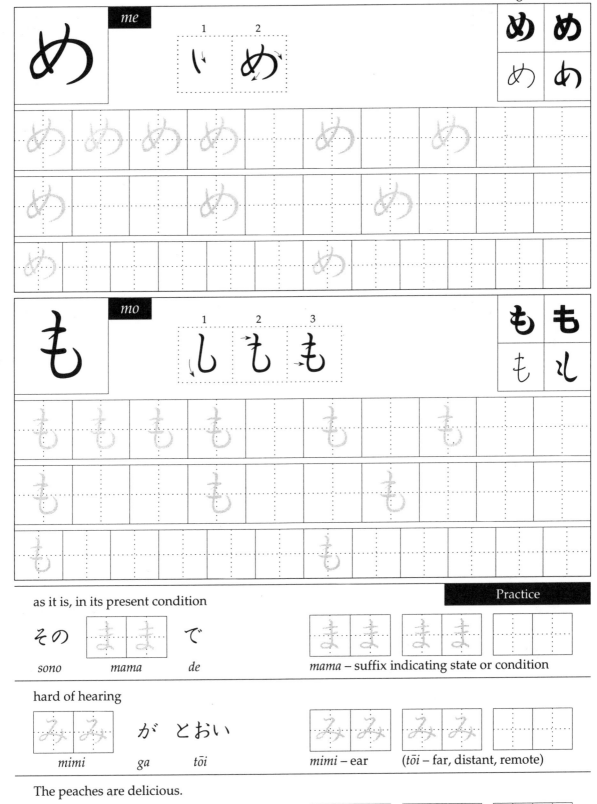

as it is, in its present condition

その ま ま で

sono   *mama*   *de*

mama – suffix indicating state or condition

hard of hearing

み み が とおい

mimi   *ga*   *tōi*

mimi – ear   (*tōi* – far, distant, remote)

The peaches are delicious.

も も は おいしい。

Momo   *wa*   *oishī.*

momo – peach

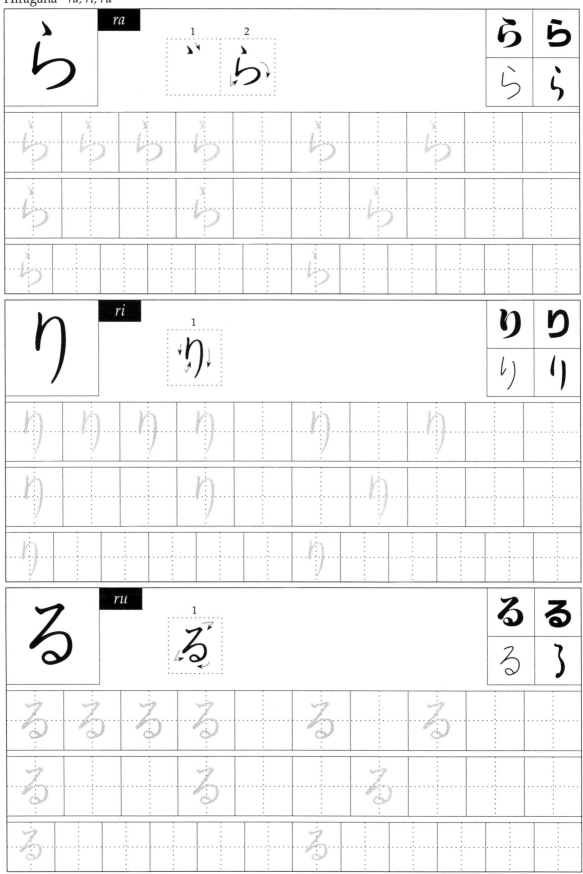

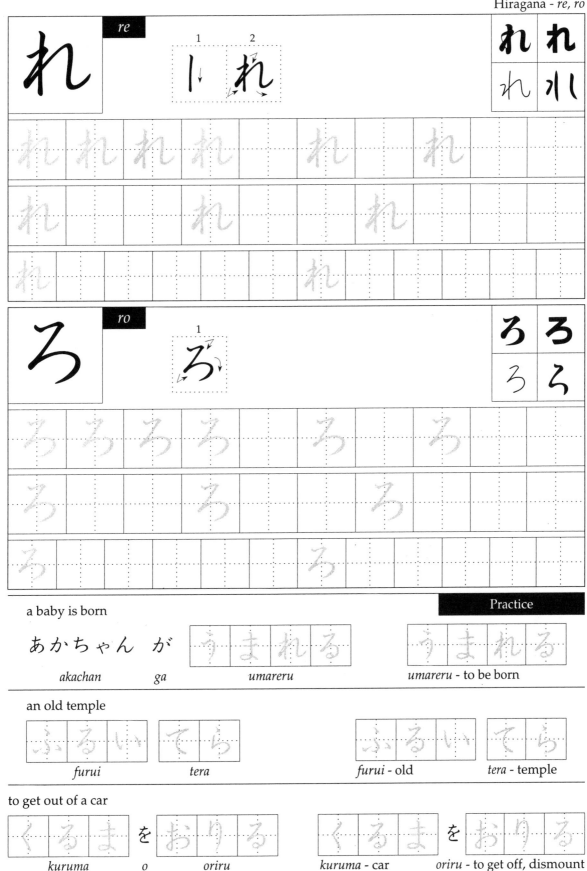

re

ro

a baby is born

あかちゃん が | う ま れ る
akachan | ga | umareru

Practice

う ま れ る
umareru - to be born

an old temple

ふ る い | て ら
furui | *tera*

ふ る い | て ら
furui - old | *tera* - temple

to get out of a car

く る ま を お り る
kuruma | *o* | *oriru*

く る ま を お り る
kuruma - car | *oriru* - to get off, dismount

29

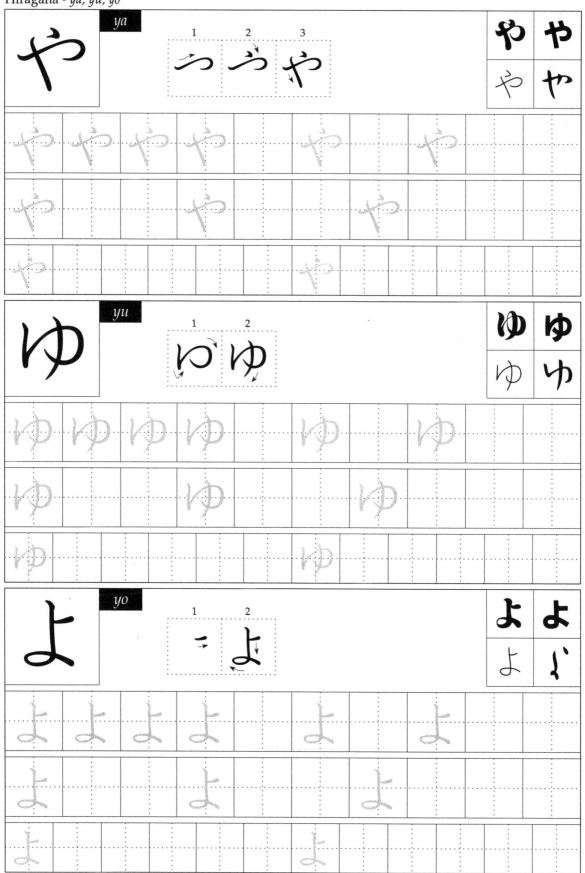

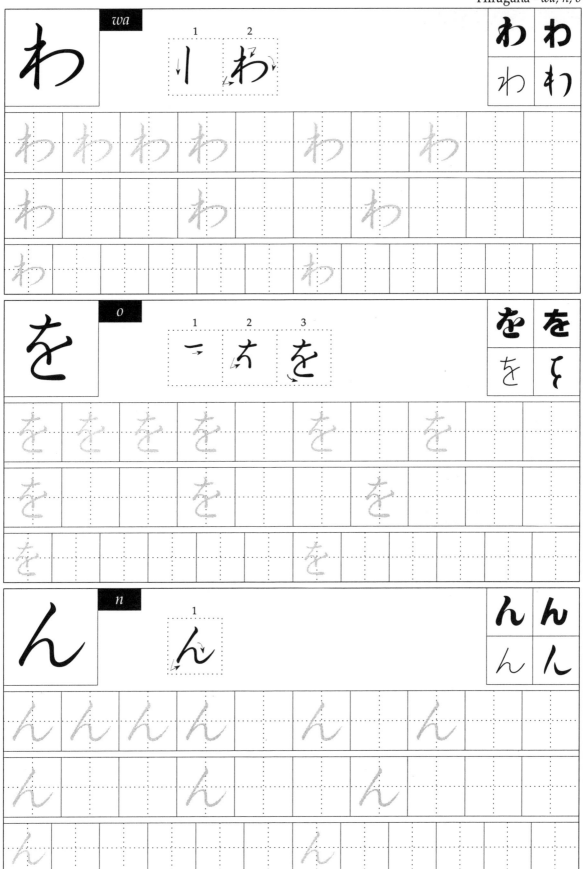

I read books every day.

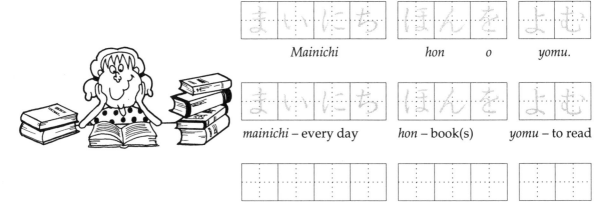

まいにち　ほんを　よむ

Mainichi　　*hon*　*o*　*yomu.*

まいにち　ほんを　よむ

mainichi – every day　　*hon* – book(s)　　*yomu* – to read

The bullet train is fast.

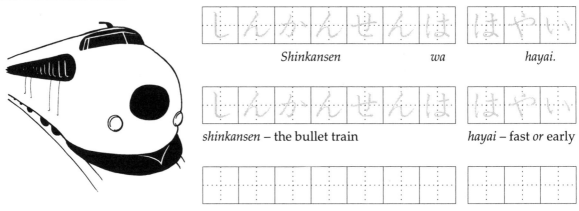

しんかんせんは　はやい

Shinkansen　　*wa*　　*hayai.*

しんかんせんは　はやい

shinkansen – the bullet train　　*hayai* – fast *or* early

The bear lives in the mountains.

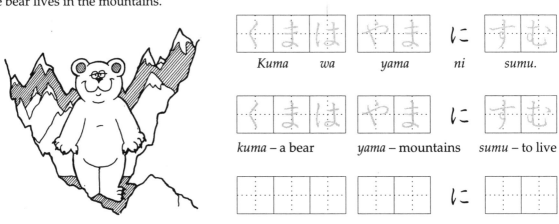

くまは　やま　に　すむ

Kuma　*wa*　*yama*　*ni*　*sumu.*

くまは　やま　に　すむ

kuma – a bear　　*yama* – mountains　　*sumu* – to live

に

I'll buy some vegetables at the vegetable store.

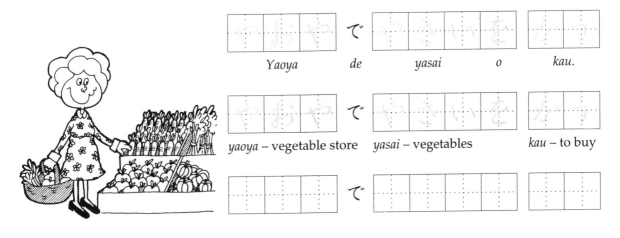

Yaoya   *de*   *yasai*   *o*   *kau.*

yaoya – vegetable store   *yasai* – vegetables   *kau* – to buy

---

Ms. Yamaha is famous.

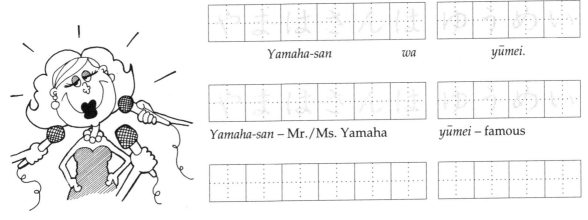

Yamaha-san   *wa*   *yūmei.*

Yamaha-san – Mr./Ms. Yamaha   *yūmei* – famous

The cars have stopped.

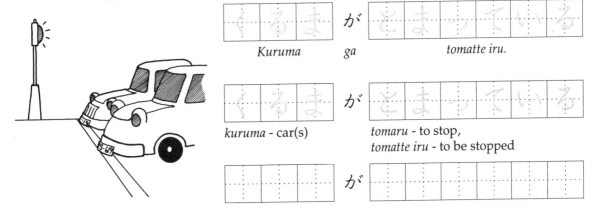

Kuruma   *ga*   *tomatte iru.*

kuruma - car(s)   *tomaru* - to stop,
tomatte iru - to be stopped

33

Of the forty-six basic hiragana characters, some begin with a voiced consonant such as 'n' or 'm', while others begin with an unvoiced consonant such as 'h' or 'k'.

The characters that begin with an unvoiced consonant have voiced counterparts, as shown in the list below. The voiced characters are known as *dakuon*, meaning 'hardened sound.'

Dakuon are denoted by two small strokes at the top right-hand side of the character.

In addition to the *dakuon*, the characters *ha, hi, fu, he,* and *ho* have the semi-voiced counterparts, *pa, pi, pu, pe,* and *po*, denoted by a small circle at the top right-hand side of the character. The semi-voiced characters are known as *handakuon*, meaning 'half-hardened sound.'

Basic Hiragana
Gojūon
ごじゅうおん

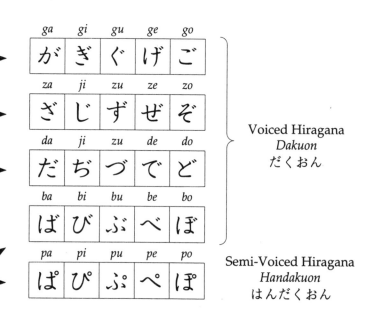

a	i	u	e	o
あ	い	う	え	お

ka	ki	ku	ke	ko
か	き	く	け	こ

sa	shi	su	se	so
さ	し	す	せ	そ

ta	chi	tsu	te	to
た	ち	つ	て	と

na	ni	nu	ne	no
な	に	ぬ	ね	の

ha	hi	fu	he	ho
は	ひ	ふ	へ	ほ

ma	mi	mu	me	mo
ま	み	む	め	も

ya		yu		yo
や		ゆ		よ

ra	ri	ru	re	ro
ら	り	る	れ	ろ

wa		o		n
わ		を		ん

ga	gi	gu	ge	go
が	ぎ	ぐ	げ	ご

za	ji	zu	ze	zo
ざ	じ	ず	ぜ	ぞ

da	ji	zu	de	do
だ	ぢ	づ	で	ど

ba	bi	bu	be	bo
ば	び	ぶ	べ	ぼ

Voiced Hiragana
Dakuon
だくおん

pa	pi	pu	pe	po
ぱ	ぴ	ぷ	ぺ	ぽ

Semi-Voiced Hiragana
Handakuon
はんだくおん

The syllable *ka* is unvoiced in *kakkō* (shape, appearnace), but voiced in *gakkō* (school).

kakkō – shape, appearance

か	っ	こ	う

gakkō – school

が	っ	こ	う

In addition to the charcters on the adjacent page, there is a set of contracted sounds.

The contracted sounds are formed by combining characters that have the 'i' sound (*ki, shi, chi, ni, hi, mi,* and *ri*) with *ya, yu* or *yo*, as shown below. The resultant contraction is pronounced as a single syllable, and is written with the second character (*ya, yu* or *yo*) smaller than the preceding character.

The contracted sounds are called *yōon*, meaning 'shortened sound'. Like the basic hiragana, the contracted sounds have voiced and semi-voiced counterparts.

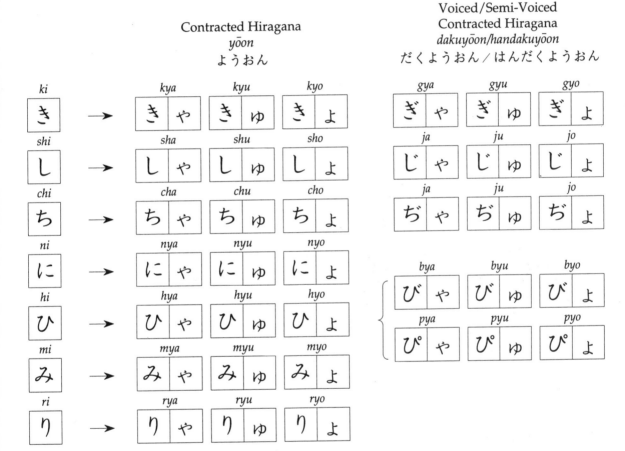

The syllables *bi* and *yo* occur as separate, uncontracted sounds in *biyōin* (beauty parlor), but as contracted sounds in *byōin* (hospital).

biyōin – beauty parlor

び	よ	う	い	ん

byōin – hospital

び	ょ	う	い	ん

The goldfish swim.

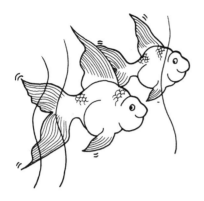

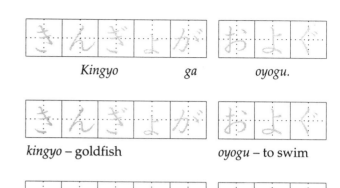

きんぎょが およぐ

Kingyo   *ga*   *oyogu.*

きんぎょが およぐ

kingyo – goldfish   *oyogu* – to swim

Just a moment!

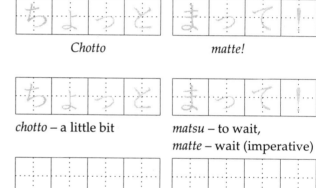

ちょっと まって！

Chotto   *matte!*

ちょっと まって！

chotto – a little bit   *matsu* – to wait,
matte – wait (imperative)

I drink the milk.

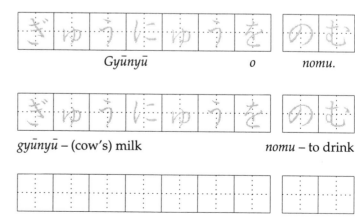

ぎゅうにゅうを のむ

Gyūnyū   *o*   *nomu.*

ぎゅうにゅうを のむ

gyūnyū – (cow's) milk   *nomu* – to drink

A train ticket

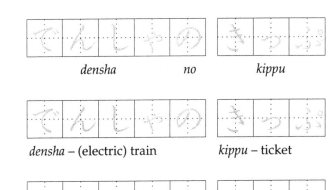

でんしゃの きっぷ

densha   *no*   *kippu*

でんしゃの きっぷ

densha – (electric) train   *kippu* – ticket

A classroom

がっこうの きょうしつ

gakkō   *no*   *kyōshitsu*

がっこうの きょうしつ

gakkō – school   *kyōshitsu* – classroom

Eight hundred and nineteen

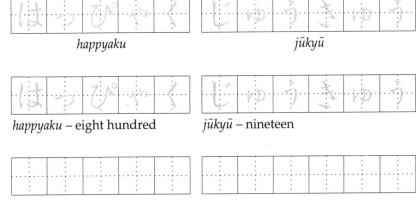

はっぴゃく じゅうきゅう

happyaku   *jūkyū*

はっぴゃく じゅうきゅう

happyaku – eight hundred   *jūkyū* – nineteen

$$800 +$$
$$10$$
$$9$$
$$\overline{819}$$

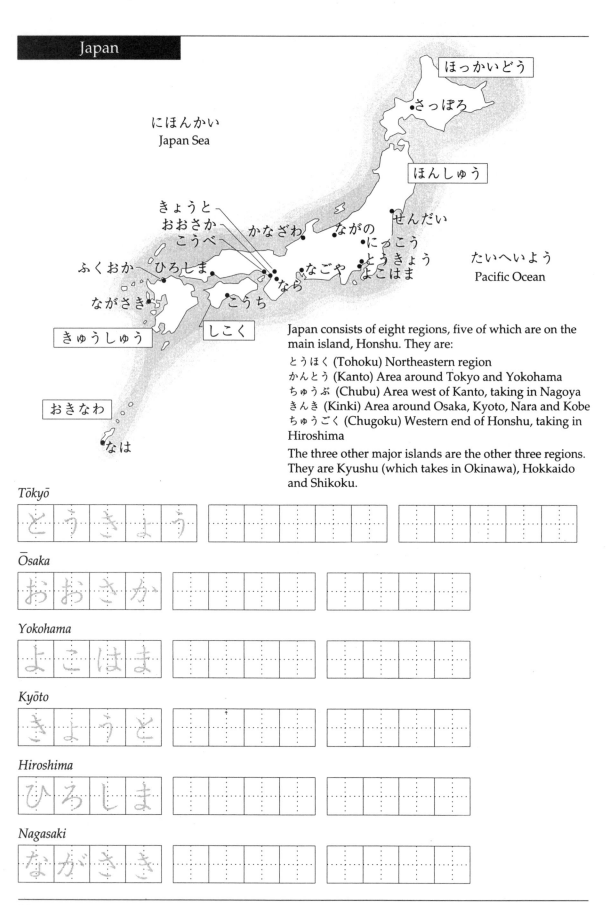

にほんかい
Japan Sea

ほっかいどう

・さっぽろ

ほんしゅう

きょうと
おおさか
こうべ
かなざわ
ながの
せんだい
にっこう
とうきょう
よこはま

たいへいよう
Pacific Ocean

ふくおか
ひろしま
なごや

ながさき
なら
こうち

きゅうしゅう
しこく

おきなわ
なは

Japan consists of eight regions, five of which are on the main island, Honshu. They are:

とうほく (Tohoku) Northeastern region
かんとう (Kanto) Area around Tokyo and Yokohama
ちゅうぶ (Chubu) Area west of Kanto, taking in Nagoya
きんき (Kinki) Area around Osaka, Kyoto, Nara and Kobe
ちゅうごく (Chugoku) Western end of Honshu, taking in Hiroshima

The three other major islands are the other three regions. They are Kyushu (which takes in Okinawa), Hokkaido and Shikoku.

Tōkyō

とうきょう

Ōsaka

おおさか

Yokohama

よこはま

Kyōto

きょうと

Hiroshima

ひろしま

Nagasaki

ながさき

Nikkō

にっこう

Fukuoka

ふくおか

Kanazawa

かなざわ

Sendai

せんだい

Nagoya

なごや

Kōbe

こうべ

Nagano

ながの

Nara

なら

Hokkaidō

ほっかいどう

Honshū

ほんしゅう

Shikoku

しこく

Kyūshū

きゅうしゅう

The clock goes ticktock, ticktock.

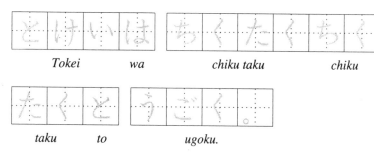

Tokei   *wa*   *chiku taku*   *chiku*

taku   *to*   *ugoku.*

tokei – clock, *ugoku* – to move

I drink the water, gulp, gulp, gulp.

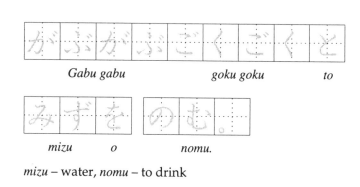

Gabu gabu   *goku goku*   *to*

mizu   *o*   *nomu.*

mizu – water, *nomu* – to drink

I eat the rice, gobble, gobble, gobble.

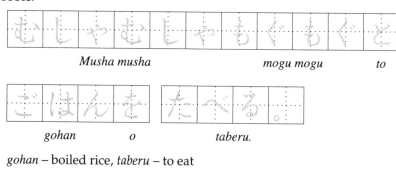

Musha musha   *mogu mogu*   *to*

gohan   *o*   *taberu.*

gohan – boiled rice, *taberu* – to eat

I've caught a cold, atchoo!

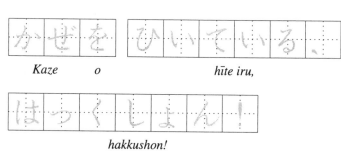

Kaze   *o*   *hīte iru,*

hakkushon!

kaze o hiku – to catch a cold
kaze o hīte iru – to have caught a cold

The cow in the field goes moo.

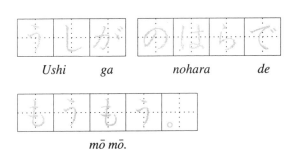

Ushi   ga   nohara   de

mō mō.

ushi – cow/bull, *nohara* – field, meadow

The mouse squeaks in its hole.

Nezumi   ga   ana   kara

chū chū.

nezumi – mouse/rat, *ana* – hole, *kara* – from

The cat goes meow.

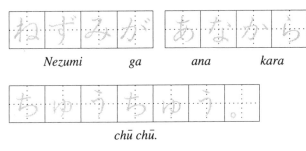

Neko   ga   nyā nyā

to   naku.

neko – cat, *naku* – to cry, chirp, squawk, bleat, croak, neigh, etc.

The frog croaks.

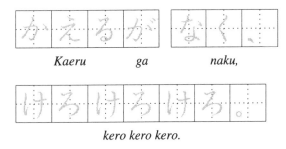

Kaeru   ga   naku,

kero kero kero.

kaeru – frog

kyōshitsu – classroom

きょうしつ

sensei – teacher

せんせい

seito – pupil, student

せいと

tsukue – desk

つくえ

tokei – clock

とけい

otokonoko – boy

おとこのこ

onnanoko – girl

おんなのこ

randoseru – knapsack, schoolbag

らんどせる

e – picture

え

Labels in illustration: きょうしつ　え　こくばん　ほん　はな　よいこ　せいと　つくえ　らんどせる　いす　おとこのこ　ものさし

hon – book
ほん

isu – chair
いす

hana – flower
はな

bōshi – cap
ぼうし

megane – glasses
めがね

enpitsu – pencil
えんぴつ

...ko – good child
...いこ

...uiko – naughty child
...るいこ

...odachi – friend(s)
...もだち

kokuban – blackboard
こくばん

monosashi – ruler
ものさし

gomibako – rubbish bin, garbage can
ごみばこ

Home

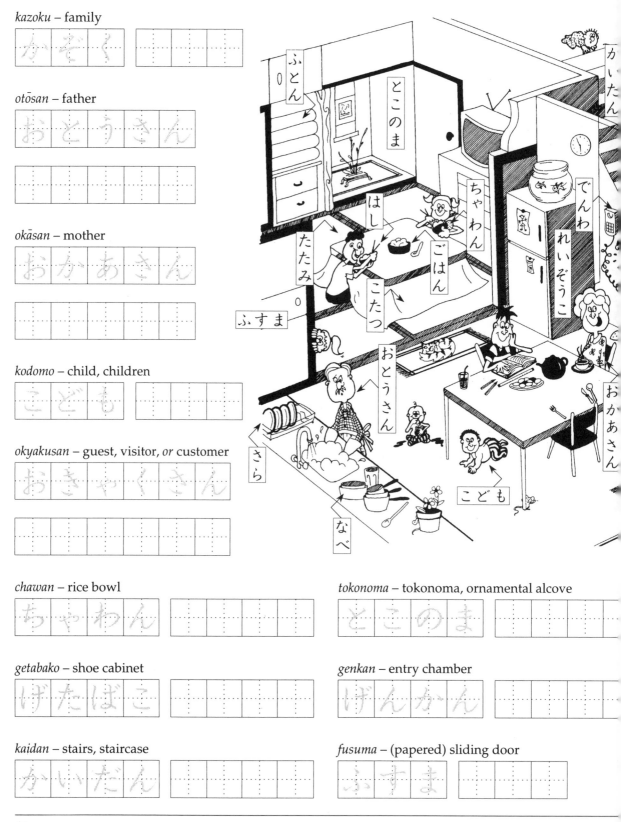

kazoku – family

かぞく

otōsan – father

おとうさん

okāsan – mother

おかあさん

kodomo – child, children

こども

okyakusan – guest, visitor, *or* customer

おきゃくさん

chawan – rice bowl

ちゃわん

tokonoma – tokonoma, ornamental alcove

とこのま

getabako – shoe cabinet

げたばこ

genkan – entry chamber

げんかん

kaidan – stairs, staircase

かいだん

fusuma – (papered) sliding door

ふすま

Labels in illustration: ふとん, とこのま, かいだん, はし, ちゃわん, でんわ, たたみ, ごはん, れいぞうこ, こたつ, ふすま, おとうさん, さら, なべ, こども, おかあさん

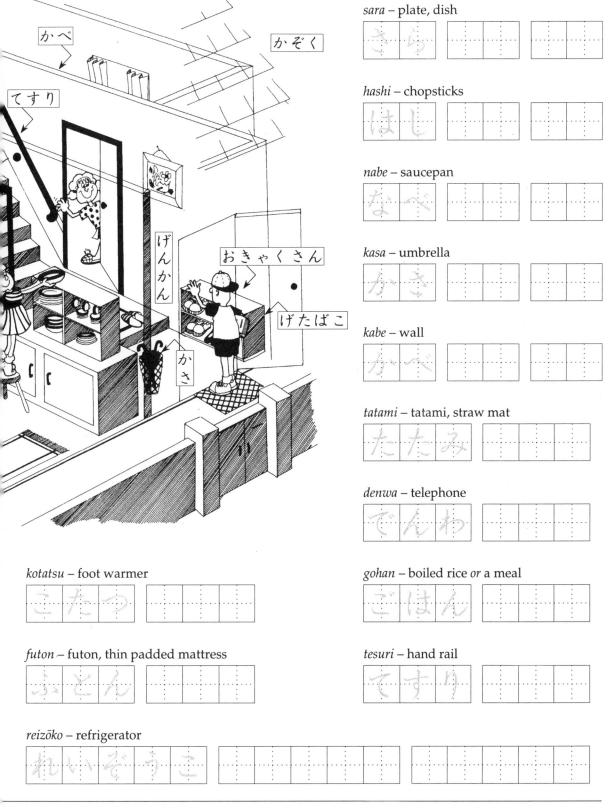

かべ

かぞく

てすり

げんかん

おきゃくさん

げたばこ

かさ

sara – plate, dish

さ ら

hashi – chopsticks

は し

nabe – saucepan

な べ

kasa – umbrella

か さ

kabe – wall

か べ

tatami – tatami, straw mat

た た み

denwa – telephone

で ん わ

kotatsu – foot warmer

こ た つ

futon – futon, thin padded mattress

ふ と ん

reizōko – refrigerator

れ い ぞ う こ

gohan – boiled rice *or* a meal

ご は ん

tesuri – hand rail

て す り

Pen Pals

Haruka Watanabe is taking her summer vacation in a popular resort near Tokyo. She has written the following letter to her friend, Akira Hashimoto. Copy the letter into the space provided.

あきらくん、おげんきですか。
わたしはげんきです。
なつやすみはたのしいですか。
わたしはうみにきています。
まいにちおよいでいます。
うみはとてもきれいです。
さようなら。
8がつ11にち
はるかより

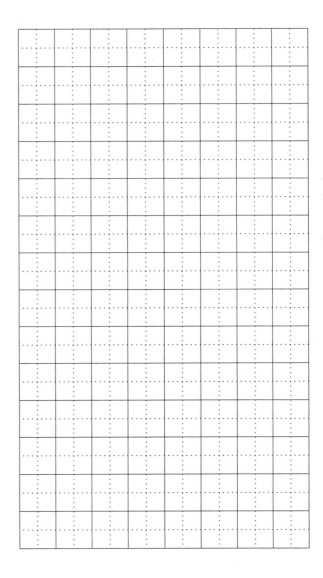

Vocabulary

kun – boy's honorific suffix
ogenki – vigor, vitality (polite)
watashi – I
genki – vigor, vitality
natsu – summer
yasumi – holiday, vacation
tanoshī – fun, pleasurable
kuru – to come
kite iru/kite imasu – to have come
mainichi – every day

oyogu – to swim
oyoide iru/oyoide imasu –
    to be swimming
umi – the ocean
totemo – very, to great degree
kirei – pretty, clean
sayonara – farewell
gatsu – month
nichi – day
chan – girl's honorific suffix

tegami – letter
otegami – letter (polite)
arigatō – thank you
boku – I (used by young males)
~mo – ~ too
hanabi – fireworks
taikai – festival
ashita – tomorrow
iku/ikimasu – to go
suki – to like